On the Waterfront

Acknowledgements:

Ian Ayris is a member of the Tyne and Wear Countywide Specialist
Conservation Team based in the Planning Division of the City of
Newcastle upon Tyne Development Department. The contribution
and assistance of the Specialist Conservation Team and the
Development Department is gratefully acknowledged.

Patricia Sheldon is a Librarian in the Local Studies Section of
Newcastle Central Library.

All photographs are copyright of Newcastle upon Tyne
City Libraries Local Studies Section, except for Nos. 13, 23, 26, 33,
45, 47 which are copyright of City Repro, No. 17 which is copyright
of Gateshead Libraries & Arts, and No. 76 which is copyright of
Patricia Sheldon.

The cover illustration is reproduced from *Quayside, Newcastle upon
Tyne* by Niels Lund, © Laing Art Gallery, Newcastle upon Tyne
(Tyne & Wear Museums Service).

The engravings are reproduced from *1800 Woodcuts by Thomas
Bewick and his School*, Dover Publications, 1962.

The map cartouche is drawn from engravings, as above.
The River-god Tyne depicted on the cartouche is the colophon of
Hindson Print Ltd.

ISBN: 1 85795 066 6

Cataloguing in Publication Data: A CIP record for this book is available from the British Library.

On the Waterfront

An historical tour of Newcastle's Quayside

by

Ian Ayris and Patricia Sheldon

Newcastle upon Tyne City Libraries & Arts

CONTENTS

ILLUSTRATIONS

The Quayside from Gateshead, 1893.

INTRODUCTION

Until the decline in the economic importance of the River Tyne in the years following the end of the Second World War, Newcastle's Quayside area had been at the heart of the growth and development of the city as both a regionally and nationally important location. The origins of the Quayside lay in the origins of the town itself, for the two are inextricably linked. The formation of the settlement known as Pons Aelius was based initially upon the Roman river crossing. The later growth of the town as an important trading port developed partly from these origins but also as a result of the topography of the dramatic Tyne Gorge and the geological strata of the surrounding land. On both sides of the river the land climbs steadily and rapidly over 250 feet. The valley sides are at their steepest immediately behind the riverside. This terrain led to the concentration of the early town around the river and in time led to the notoriously overcrowded living conditions which survived near the Quayside until the nineteenth century.

The post-medieval economic development of both the Quayside and the town of Newcastle was based on coal – initially through the mining of the outcropping seams in the river valley but later by the wholesale exploitation of the Great Northern Coalfield. The transportation of this vital fuel became the lifeblood of the river. In time not only did an elaborate rail system develop to bring coal to the river but also the whole industrial basis of the region was built upon it. The development of the railways and the locomotive, the rise of the North East shipbuilding industry and the region's reputation as a centre of heavy engineering and industrial innovation were all a result of the mining and transportation of coal. The profit to be made in overcoming the obstacles presented in the navigation of the narrow, shallow channels of the River Tyne and plying the coal trade was at the centre of the growth of the town and the river – a trade which generated the national and international importance of Newcastle. By the end of the seventeenth century 90 per cent of the ships leaving the port carried coal to London and other British ports as well as European markets. For many centuries ships on their return journey to the Tyne carried only ballast. A number of industries, notably the pottery industry, grew up utilising the chalk and flint contained within the ballast stone. On occasion some items of use were carried as ballast, clay roofing pantiles being one example. By the early eighteenth century, however, ships began to bring in the many and varied cargoes which fostered and supported the development of the thriving town and port of Newcastle upon Tyne. The Quayside was at the centre of this bustling activity.

1. "Wasteneys' Old Place", c1885, one of the many yards and entries off The Close, often named after their occupiers. Wasteneys Smith set up an engineering firm at 39, The Close in 1871 and gained immediate success by patenting a stockless anchor. The founder, William Wasteneys Smith, had been a bridge inspector employed by the Russian government on the Caucasian Railway. The firm opened premises in the Sandhill c1881 and eventually moved out of Newcastle to a site at Killingworth in 1965. The term "Wasteneys' Old Place" presumably came into use when the firm moved to 58-60 Sandhill.

THE CLOSE

The Close developed on land reclaimed from the river between the thirteenth and fifteenth centuries by the tipping of rubbish behind successive waterfronts. From this time it became colonised by merchants, burgesses and members of the aristocracy.

On the north side of the road there was building space only on narrow strips of level ground at the foot of the steep slope. On the south side, however, land reclamation allowed buildings to be longer and narrower and enabled their extension to the river edge for the loading and unloading of goods. An example of this type of medieval merchant's house survives at 35, The Close, now converted to a restaurant. Among the most prestigious buildings on the south side of The Close was the Mansion House, built in 1691-2, which acted as the Mayor's residence and the venue for elaborate dinners and balls.

The Close remained a prosperous quarter of the town until it began to decline in the early eighteenth century. In 1736 the historian Henry Bourne observed that "Of late Years these Houses have been forsaken, and their wealthier Inhabitants have chosen the higher Parts of the Town". In their place industry grew up. The Mansion House was abandoned in 1835 and used as a warehouse until it was destroyed by fire in 1895, its role having been taken over by the property at 1, Ellison Place. Of the industrial concerns which developed along The Close one of the most significant was the Phoenix Flour Mill. Built in the mid-nineteenth century, it became the home of the now famous Spiller's Company who remodelled the mill when they moved from Bridgwater in Somerset to Newcastle in 1896.

3. Long Stairs, leading from The Close to Queen's Lane, 1924.

2. (left) The yard of the Queen's Head Hotel on September 8th 1907. The public house shared the address of 39, The Close with Wasteneys Smith. It is first mentioned in local directories here in c1879 when the innkeeper was A. Brown.

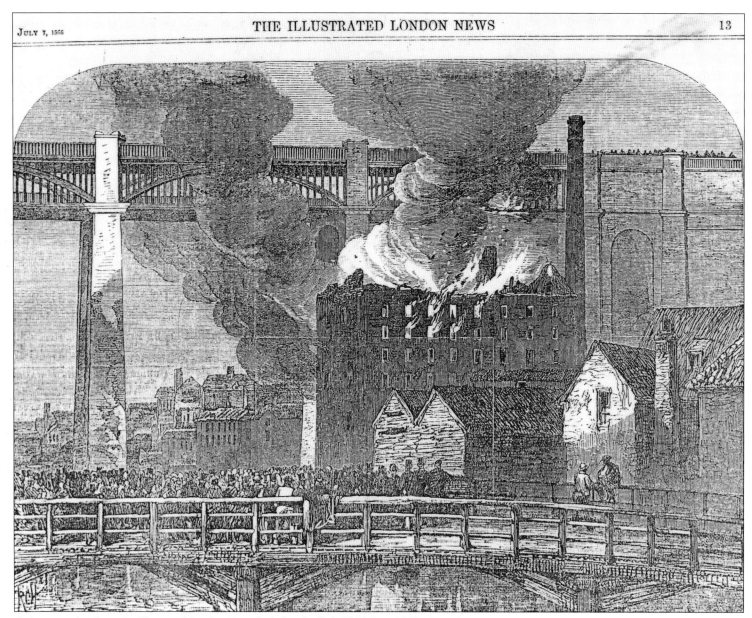

4. An engraving from the *Illustrated London News* depicting the fire of 24th June 1866.

THE HIGH LEVEL BRIDGE

Towering above The Close is the oldest of Newcastle's surviving river bridges. The impressive stature of the High Level Bridge, designed and engineered by Robert Stephenson and Thomas Harrison, was constructed between 1845 and 1849. Its design was the conclusion of a long period of suggestions and proposals by some of the leading engineers and architects of the day, including not only John Dobson but also the great Isambard Kingdom Brunel. When completed the bridge was a vitally important link in the region's railway network, bringing trains across the Tyne and into Newcastle's newly built Central Station. The bridge stands 120ft (36.5m) above low water and has an overall length of 1,400ft (425.6m). The two tiered bridge is now a Grade One Listed Building and to this day carries rail traffic on the upper deck and road traffic on the lower deck. With the demise of the upper rail deck of the Queen Alexandra Bridge across the River Wear the "High Level" is the region's only twin deck bridge.

5. The High Level Bridge prior to the removal of the eighteenth-century Tyne Bridge in 1866.

TER DUE.　　　　　　　　SATURDAY, JUNE 30, 1866.　　　REGISTERED FOR TRANSMISSION ABROAD　　PRICE 2D.

FIRE AT THE HIGH-LEVEL BRIDGE, NEWCASTLE

A GREAT fire, which destroyed property valued at £70,000, took place on Sunday the 24th ult., at Newcastle-on-Tyne. It was in Mr. Brown's steam flour-mill, a building of six stories, situated on the quay, directly under the High-level Bridge. The lowest story was occupied by Mr. Van Hansbergen, as a warehouse for nitrate of soda. On the Saturday night, the mill being very busy, some of the men worked until three in the morning, when they left the premises. At eight in the morning it was found that a number of packs of flour were on fire. Before these could be removed all the lower part of the building was filled with flame. The workmen were called together, and the North British fire brigade soon arrived but the conflagration had by this time reached the second story. The nitrate of soda was removed, however, from the cellars in boats, and some bags of flour were thrown down from the upper floors, by men who ventured to ascend for that purpose. Thousands of people gathered on the old Tyne Bridge to get a view of the fire, which raged with terrific fury. It was feared that there might be an explosion, as it was known that there was a considerable quantity of naphtha and other explosive materials bonded to The Close, at no very considerable distance from the burning mill. The third and fourth stories of the building took fire, and by half past ten o'clock every part of the interior of the mill was in flames, and a few minutes afterwards the roof fell in with a crash. The floors of the several stories also fell in, and the ponderous machinery was thrown to the ground. Immediately after the roof had fallen the draught which followed it and the wind from the south-east sent the flames up against the already hot wood at the bottom of the High-level Bridge, and the result was that the bridge took fire. The railway authorities immediately collected a number of men with crowbars, chisels, and sledge hammers, to rip up the asphalt and timbers of the side path of the bridge for a length of eighty or one hundred yards, while through the breaches in the pathway water was poured in, which seemed, however, to have little effect. The body of the flames could not be touched, and the seething and boiling pitch on the carriage-way told that the conflagration had got fair hold of the whole flooring structure between the massive stone buttresses. The superintendents or managers of the railway company and the fire brigade consulted, and determined that water should be thrown over the burning rafters from beneath. This, however, seemed rather hazardous, and there might have been a difficulty had not a few of the Newcastle Naval Reserve been near. Four boatswains' chairs were rigged; on these John Stubbs, assistant to the harbour-master at Shields; Henry Wilson, Thomas Forsyth, and George Bolton, three of the Newcastle Naval Reserve, took their places and were lowered over the parapet of the bridge, with instructions to erect a platform from the parapet on which some one might stand and play on the burning timbers. This was done with the aid of the police, and thus a hold was got upon the flames. Long after the mill had been destoyed, and the fire almost quenched in that quarter, the bridge continued to burn in some part, but no fears were entertained for the safety of the noble structure. The most that was apprehended was the burning of the woodwork.

From the *Illustrated London News*

6. Mylne's stone-built Tyne Bridge photographed in the early 1860s.

THE TYNE BRIDGES

A bridge has crossed the Tyne since at least the 2nd century. Although the precise location of the Roman bridge is uncertain, Roman objects, such as a coin from the reign of Hadrian dating from AD 132-4, have been dredged from the river in the vicinity of the modern Swing Bridge.

A new bridge was built across the Tyne, probably in the late twelfth century, on what is thought to have been the site of the Roman bridge. This medieval bridge is said to have had twelve arches, of which three were land arches. It was defended by three towers and on it, toward the southern end, was the Blue Stone which marked the boundary between Newcastle and the Palatinate of Durham. The bridge survived until 17th November 1771 when the great flood on the Tyne swept away four of the arches.

The medieval bridge was replaced by a sturdy stone bridge of nine arches with fine masonry and elegant balustrades. However, within a century it was recognised as a serious obstacle to the prosperity of the river. The inability of anything other than the smallest boats to pass upstream of the bridge not only allowed the Tyne keelmen to maintain their stranglehold on the movement of coal on the river but also prejudiced the development of the river banks to the west of the quayside. This factor was of particular significance to William Armstrong, whose industrial empire at Elswick was restricted by this drawback. As a consequence the old bridge was replaced firstly by a temporary wooden bridge and then by the Tyne Swing Bridge.

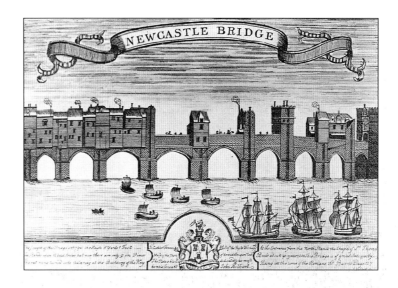

7. The medieval Tyne Bridge before and after the destructive flood of 1771. The illustration above dates from 1727 and shows the houses and shops on the bridge. The engraving below depicts the bridge in 1772 after the deluge of the previous year.

8. The first class dreadnought *Superb* passing through the Swing Bridge after its launch at the Elswick Shipyard on 6th November 1907.

THE SWING BRIDGE

Built by W. G. Armstrong & Co., the Tyne Swing Bridge opened in 1876. The moving central span is still operated by Armstrong's hydraulic machinery, although the steam pumps have been replaced by electric ones. The turning bridge allowed shipping traffic to travel up river and in its busiest year, 1924, more than 6,000 ships passed through. Now the bridge opens rarely. In its time, however, the bridge has been a major influence on the history of the river. By allowing access to the upper reaches for large sea-going vessels the industrial development of the north and south banks of the river beyond the centres of Newcastle and Gateshead was facilitated. Armstrong's works at Elswick expanded rapidly following the combination of the construction of the bridge and the dredging and improving of the river channels by the Tyne Improvement Commission. Armstrong was now able not only to arm ships built at other yards but also construct ships within his own yard, developed as part of the works complex in the 1870s. Whilst the Elswick Works have now disappeared, one of the major constructions on the south bank, the Dunston Staiths, built by the NER at the turn of the century, survives to this day and, like the Swing Bridge itself, is a Scheduled Ancient Monument.

9. (above) Swing Bridge at 5.15 p.m. 3rd June 1924, photographed during a traffic census.

10. "Tommy on the Bridge", a blind mendicant, was a daily sight on the Tyne Swing Bridge, allegedly bestriding the mark in the centre of the bridge which indicated the boundary between Newcastle and Gateshead and thereby avoiding the authorities. Thomas Ferens is thought to have been born in 1842 in The Close. He died in severe weather on New Year's Day 1907 after collapsing in the snow at the Gateshead end of the bridge.

11. Aberdeen Wharf viewed from the Swing Bridge on the 19th November 1912.

THE QUAYSIDE

Whilst the completion of the Swing Bridge in 1876 allowed the berthing facilities of the Quayside to extend beyond the confines of the traditional bridging point, it was the work of Newcastle Corporation in the second half of the nineteenth century which extended the quay facilities eastwards to the mouth of the Ouseburn. For many centuries prior to these events, however, the Quayside stretched only from the old Tyne Bridge to Sandgate. Along the quay ran the medieval Town Wall until it was dismantled in 1763. Its removal allowed greater use of the quay and easier access to the buildings of the town. Following their development in the 1840s Armstrong's hydraulically operated cranes proliferated along the length of the quay and various wharves were established which served places both home and abroad.

"Nowadays", said the historian Charleton in 1885, "it is the Aberdeen boat which moors opposite the Guildhall, on which occasions the quay becomes covered with a heaped-up mass of merchandise; steam cranes puff and snort; stevedores' labourers work like slaves, unshipping and shipping cargo; carts and horses come and go in long trains, till at last the quay is clear again, the blue peter is hoisted, the Countess of Aberdeen cuts loose her moorings and steams off again on her way to the Granite City".

12. Part of Buck's View of the Quayside in 1745 showing the Town Wall along the river's edge.

NEWCASTLE AND ABERDEEN.—The COUNTESS OF ABERDEEN (or other steamer) is intended to leave Newcastle every Wednesday Afternoon, and Aberdeen every Saturday Afternoon, unless prevented by the weather or unforeseen circumstances.
Fares:—First Cabin, 10s; Second Cabin, 6s.   Return Tickets: First Cabin, 15s: Second Cabin, 7s. 6d.
For further particulars, apply to WILLIAM SKIRVING, 22, Regent Quay, Aberdeen; or JOHN N. MOULD, 57, Quayside, Newcastle-on-Tyne.

From the *Newcastle Daily Journal*, February 18th, 1885.

13. The elegant former fish market, built in 1880 to the design of A.M. Fowler. Used for many years for cold storage by Sansinena, it has now been converted to form prestigious offices. The building retains many of its original features, including the statues of Neptune and fish wives.

14. Market stalls near the Sandhill in about 1915. In 1885 Charleton described the area as "occupied by stalls with gaily covered awnings, mostly owned by vendors of ice cream."

SANDHILL

In the reign of Richard II a Proclamation was made commanding the removal of all merchandise from the "Common Place, in Newcastle called Sandhill, where the Inhabitants were wont to assemble for their Recreation."

"The Sandhill" wrote Henry Bourne in 1736 "is so called because it was formerly a Hill of naked Sand, when the tide was out. For formerly the Tyne overflowed all this Place … It is a spacious Place and adorned with Buildings very high and stately, whose Rooms speak the Ancient Grandeur, being very large and Magnificent. It is now that Part of the Town where the chief Affairs of Trade and Business are transacted. The Shops in this Street are almost altogether those of Merchants, which have many of them great Conveniences of Lofts, Garners and Cellars. Here is the Market for Fish, Herbs, Bread, Cloth, Leather, etc…"

As well as the houses and shops of merchants, such as Bessie Surtees House, the major public buildings of the developing town were built here. The original Town Hall or Exchange was constructed here, as was the Guildhall. A statue of James II was erected here and later torn down and hurled into the river. Like The Close, however, the area declined in prosperity as the urban aristocracy moved away from the increasingly squalid Quayside area. While the original Town Hall was demolished, the Guildhall was rebuilt in the 1650s and, although altered over the years, survives to this day. The addition of the collonaded fish market in 1823, designed by John Dobson, ended the need to have the numerous fish stalls which previously crowded the quay. Fishing boats continued to bring their catch to the heart of the Quayside until much later in the century, as the historian Charleton noted in 1885.

"Here, not so long ago, the 'Five man boats' with their load of freshly caught north sea fish, made fast alongside, while on the quay stood crowds of bare-headed, bare-armed, kilted-skirted, white-aproned women, with round shallow baskets and twisted 'weazes' in their hands, ready to crowd on board as a soon as a plank was laid ashore."

15. Sandhill in 1897 showing the Ye Old Queen Elizabeth inn, a survivor of the Quayside fire of 1854.

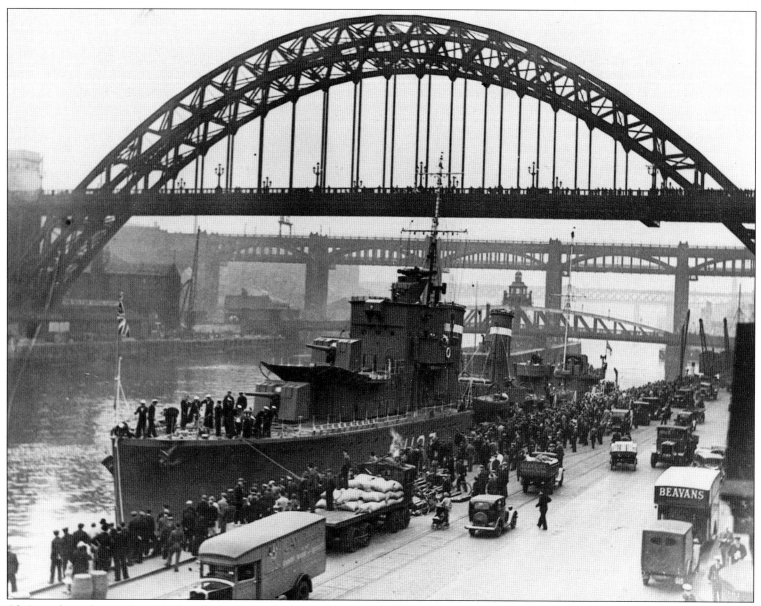

16. A naval vessel moored near the Tyne Bridge attracted a throng of spectators in 1936.

THE TYNE BRIDGE

The building of the Tyne Bridge was a dominant factor in the eventual decline of the Quayside as an important element in the commercial life of the city. Bestriding the river, dominating the Quayside, it whisked traffic directly into the new heart of the city.

The gradual movement away from the lower parts of the town begun in the late seventeenth and eighteenth centuries had developed into the building of Dobson and Grainger's new town centre in the nineteenth. The High Level Bridge allowed both rail and road traffic to avoid the Quayside. However, overcrowding and delays ensured a constant vehicle usage of the Swing Bridge and the roads along the Quayside.

The new Tyne Bridge, built by Dorman, Long & Co. of Middlesbrough to a design by Mott, Hay and Anderson and opened in 1928, allowed even easier access into the higher parts of the town. The Quayside became isolated from the commercial and business activity of Newcastle.

18. The Tyne Bridge under construction in February 1928, seen by a photographer perched on the Gateshead end of the deck.

17. Sketch proposal for the architectural treatment of the piers and approach to the Tyne Bridge by R. Burns Dick, showing the grand entrance arch into the City – a facet of the scheme which did not come to fruition.

19. The Quayside two weeks before the Great Fire of 1854 …

A DIRTY AND INCONVENIENT STREET

Whilst burgeoning trade of all sorts brought an air of economic prosperity to the late eighteenth century Quayside, the movement of the moneyed classes to more commodious properties higher in the town and the gradually deteriorating medieval buildings which filled the narrow chares running off the quay brought considerable social decay. A huge variety of imported cargoes, such as wine and port from Portugal, raisins from Spain, timber from Norway, hemp and flax from Russia, corn from Danzig and brandy from France helped to make Newcastle what the historian Mackenzie called "one of the largest and most commodious wharfs in the Kingdom". However the needs of the port resulted in a heady mixture of industries, shops, warehouses, inns and houses of ill repute side by side with the dwellings of the poorer elements of the town. The area was still at the centre of the town's commercial prosperity but the Quayside itself was described by Mackenzie in 1827 as "a dirty and inconvenient street."

20....and immediately after the conflagration.

21. Salvage and demolition followed the fire, with much of the river front damaged beyond repair.

THE GREAT FIRE OF 1854

Typhus had long been endemic in the lower parts of Newcastle. Throughout the 1830s and 1840s almost 300 people a year were carried off as a result of the fever. The arrival in England of the even more terrifying cholera, which struck in three frightening epidemics in 1831-32, 1848-49 and 1853, was of even greater concern. The death toll in Newcastle in this last outbreak was 1,533 – many of whom came from the fever dens of the The Close, Quayside and Sandgate.

It was in this squalid atmosphere of crowded and dirty streets that what the newspapers of the time called "the most terrible and appalling catastrophe which ever occurred in the towns of Newcastle and Gateshead" took place. The drama began shortly after midnight on Friday 6th October 1854, when a worsted manufactory in Hillgate in Gateshead was found to be ablaze.

Strenuous efforts to extinguish the flames failed and the heat caused sulphur, stored in a neighbouring warehouse, to melt and ignite. At 3.10 a.m. a series of explosions occurred, heard as far away as Hartlepool and mistaken by the folk of Shields for an earthquake. Apart from the terrible destruction caused in Gateshead, the force of the explosions sent fireballs of blazing sulphur and other volatile substances across the river to ignite a 120 yard length of the Quayside and the area behind it. In spite of the best efforts of the fire-fighters and the Army, it was nightfall before the flames were under control and sightseers flocked to view the scenes of devastation. These events were indeed terrible for causing the loss of over fifty lives. However, countless lives may have been saved by the destruction of some of the most fever ridden alleyways and the most insanitary housing conditions in the town.

22. The aftermath of October 6th 1854.

23. The gracious buildings of the post-fire redevelopment, photographed in 1980.

REBUILDING THE QUAYSIDE

The western end of the Quayside was virtually destroyed by the great fire of 1854. Of the sixteen chares situated between the Sandhill and Broad Chare before the fire, only seven survived. However, hundreds of families were moved out of the ancient centre into the newly expanding suburbs. John Dobson, whose son Alexander had been a victim of the disaster, designed a new layout of broad streets, – King Street, Queen Street and Lombard Street – in a formalised pattern to replace the lost medieval buildings and ancient alleys.

With the removal of much of the housing the quay became a predominantly trading and commercial area. Many of the shops (there had been 33 butcher's shops on the Quayside at one time) and small industries were lost, although the inns, boarding – and bawdy-houses retained the trade of visiting seamen and merchants, as they had for hundreds of years. As Bourne noted in 1736, "It is not so much to be wondered at, if in going along it you see almost nothing but a whole Street of Sign-posts of Taverns, Ale-houses, Coffee houses, etc."

A further feature of the Victorian development of the area was the rebuilding of the quay itself. Years of neglect and the deepening of the river by the dredging work of the Tyne Improvement Commission had made the quay unstable. Between 1866 and 1884 the walls were rebuilt and the quay extended to the mouth of the Ouseburn.

24. In some cases an older building remained incongruously sandwiched between grander neighbours – in this case the premises of Septimus A. Cail, printers and stationers. Septimus Cail was born in 1820 and as a young man was the first Newcastle station master of the Newcastle and Carlisle Railway. He joined the optician's firm of his brother on the Quayside but moved into the stationery and printing business for which his firm became noted. As a prominent local businessman he was involved in a number of concerns, notably the construction of the second Redheugh Bridge. This photograph was taken in 1964.

[COPYRIGHT.]—ENTERED AT STATIONERS' HALL.   [REGISTERED FOR TRANSMISSION ABROAD.]

THE TYNE
Bill of Entry & Shipping List.
INCLUDING NEWCASTLE AND NORTH AND SOUTH SHIELDS.

Published daily under the Authority of the Directors of the Customs' Annuity and Benevolent Fund, established by Act of Parliament, 56 Geo. III., Cap. LXXIII., by C. S. Saunders, Esq., Collector of Customs, Newcastle.

PRINTED AT NEWCASTLE-UPON-TYNE, BY SEPTIMUS A. CAIL, Nos. 42 and 43, QUAYSIDE.

SUBSCRIPTION, £2 2s. PER ANNUM, PAYABLE HALF-YEARLY IN ADVANCE.

25. The Customs House stands at the centre of this photograph of the predominantly Victorian buildings of the Quayside, taken in 1973.

VICTORIAN REDEVELOPMENT

With the rebuilding of much of the Quayside in the middle of the nineteenth century a number of dominating buildings were added to the river frontage.

The Customs House had been at the centre of the Quayside since its construction in 1766. The building was refronted in 1830 to a design by Sidney Smirke. It replaced an earlier Customs House which stood at the western end of the quay. On completion of the new building the old house was used as an inn for many years.

At the centre of Dobson's new street layout was Exchange Buildings, a large stone built office block designed by William Parnell in the early 1860s. Between here and the Customs House equally impressive offices were added later in the century. Mercantile Building (Nos. 15-23) was constructed in 1883 by J.C. Parsons and Nos. 25 & 27 were built as a shop and offices by John Wardle in 1869.

To the east of the Customs House, Coronation Buildings and Baltic Chambers were developed in the early years of the twentieth century. With the exception of a small number of earlier buildings which had survived both destruction and redevelopment, in the fifty years following the fire the Quayside from Sandhill to Broad Chare was transformed.

26. No. 63, Quayside, at the time Christies Bar, and the neighbouring Coronation Buildings, pictured in 1984.

27. Broad Chare and Spicer Lane emerge onto the Quayside, here pictured in 1895. The building housing Chadburn's Telegraph Company was soon to make way for the construction of Baltic Chambers.

BROAD CHARE – NEITHER A SAFE NOR A PLEASANT PASSAGE

With the development of prestigious Victorian offices at the west end of the Quayside, Broad Chare became an informal boundary between the new business premises and the older warehouses and factories. Broad Chare itself had been one of the most prominent of the early alleyways being, as the name suggests, wider than its counterparts.

The Quayside chares had been a network of cramped alleyways. Most of the chares, according to the historian Mackenzie, could be easily spanned by the extended arms of a middle-sized man and some with a single arm. In Dark Chare the houses nearly touched each other and the thoroughfare was no longer passable. The names and spellings of the twenty lanes changed frequently. Some were named after inns in the streets, such as the The Three Indian Kings and the Black Boy Chare. Others were known for different reasons. Mackenzie reports that Plumber Chare was noted as "the receptacle of Cyprian Nymphs whose blandishments were of the most coarse and vulgar description. Indeed," he lamented "most of these dark lanes were inhabited by very dangerous though not very tempting females."

The area had nevertheless been the home of many of the influential and prosperous people of the town who had gained wealth and position in the coal trade, the name Fenwick's Entry testifying to the whereabouts of the home of Alderman Cuthbert Fenwick.

Mackenzie's description of the Quayside chares includes Broad Chare which "is broad enough to admit a cart. Most of the old houses have been pulled down and lofty commodious warehouses erected in their place. A narrow flagged foot path runs up the west side, but is neither a safe nor a pleasant passage."

28. The relatively Broad Chare in 1890.

29. "Paddy's Market" with second hand clothes laid unceremoniously on the setts at the turn of the century.

MILK MARKET

There has been a "Milk Market" at the Quayside since at least 1717. The agricultural overtones of its name bear testimony to the site of the sale of milk and other produce and of the " hirings " where agricultural workers congregated waiting to be hired by local farmers.

The bucolic picture painted by some observers had certainly disappeared by the middle of the nineteenth century. The "hirings" moved to the Westgate in 1827 and the area took on a much more prosaic appearance. An anonymous contributor to the *Northumbrian Magazine* in 1881 noted that "The name Milk Market would naturally suggest to a stranger pleasant visions of country life and all the agreeable surroundings of a farmstead, of pretty buxom milkmaids in snow-white aprons, of milk cans polished till they shine like silver. But alas ! such anticipations are woefully disappointed by the reality. It was," the reporter continued "an unsavoury locality, haggling and bargaining over the wretched rags going on all day long between the shabby buyers and the shabbier sellers ... The crumbling, decayed old buildings that look as though they only waited for a moderate gust of wind to convert them into a site of rubbish, form a fitting background to a picture such as only Dickens could ever paint ... If you should be of a meditative turn and disposed to moralise on the decay of all earthly things, we should recommend you take a stroll through that place."

The horrified moralist, clearly more at home with the splendours of Dobson and Grainger, concluded that although "the rickety old buildings may one day be swept away, the poor will always be with us!"

30. The floating wharf moored opposite the end of Broad Chare in the mid 1890s.

31. A Quayside workman taking a break from his labours in 1905.

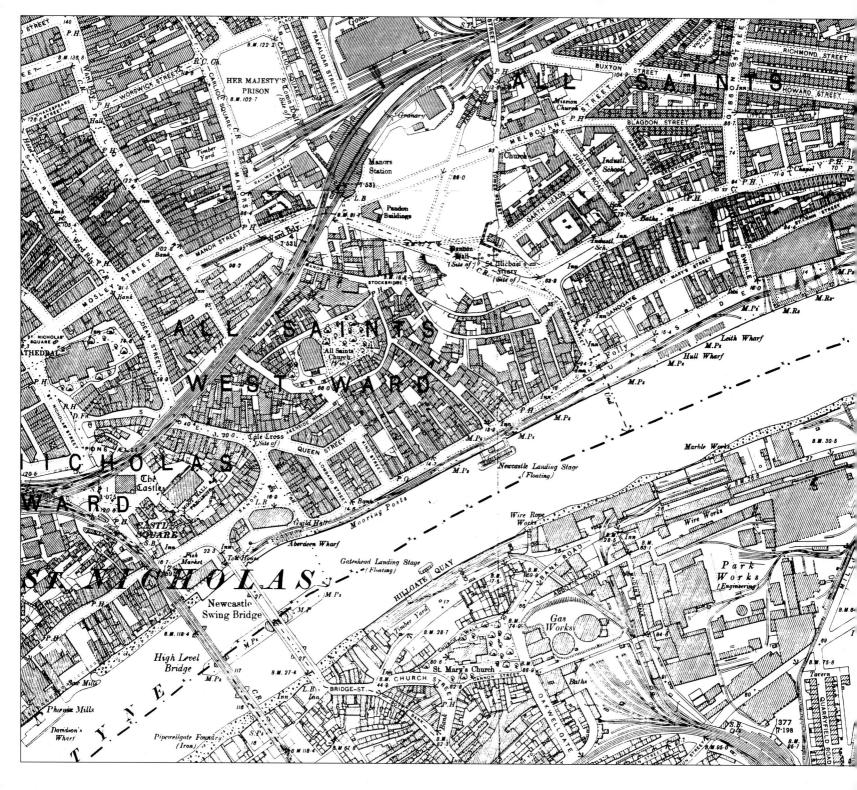

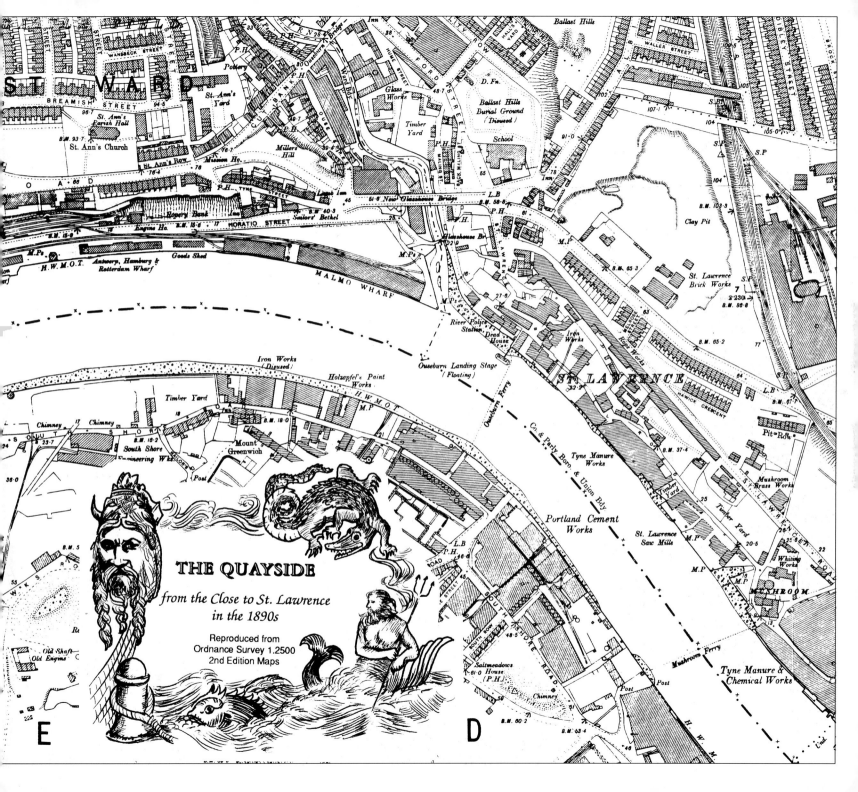

33. The Tyne public house and the Love Lane Warehouses, looking ripe for demolition in 1982, were transformed into flats and a restaurant a decade later.

WAREHOUSES

From the dawn of the nineteenth century until the late twentieth century the area between Broad Chare and the Milk Market was dominated by large purpose-built warehouses. Prior to this their construction had been achieved by adapting existing Quayside properties, particularly in the narrow chares and along Dog Bank. The new nineteenth century warehouses respected the lines of the medieval alleyways and retained the character of the area as one of high buildings and narrow lanes.

In 1801, in return for agreeing to the construction of Forster Street through property he was leasing, a man named Pollard, with considerable business interests in the area, was allowed the use of stone from the old town wall for construction. He is thought to have been responsible for a major group of warehouses built between 1801 and 1830, some of which survive to this day, converted into apartments.

The recent transformation of the eastern end of the Quayside, in particular the conversion of the impressive Love Lane warehouse with its long thirteen bay, seven storey frontage, has returned much of this area to the residential use it enjoyed over two hundred years ago. The former status of the whole Quayside as the heart of the town has also been partly restored by the return of dwellings and commerce to the area and by the construction of the awesome Crown Court building.

34. (above right) An Edwardian racing tipster pulls the crowds on the Quayside near the Milk Market.

35. (right) "Paddy's Market", little changed by the time of this photograph in 1954, continued to take place until the 1960s.

Sandgate 1890

36. Water and a street musician prove an irresistible attraction for the children of Sandgate in 1890.

WATER AND WORSE

Near the Milk Market stood many public houses, the Sandgate water pant, the Wesley memorial drinking fountain and the local midden.

At the turn of the twentieth century inns were numerous; at the foot of Spicer Lane was the Ship Inn, either side of Byker Chare were the Turks Head and the Bridge Inn, between Love Lane and Bethel Lane stood the Steamboat Inn. At the foot of the Milk Market itself was The Tyne public house and across the road, the Lifeboat Inn, whilst on the corner of Sandgate were the Portland Arms, the Grey Horse Inn and the Barley Mow Inn.

Water was provided by the Sandgate Pant, a popular gathering point at the head of the Sandgate, and later by the Wesley drinking fountain. Established in 1891 to mark the centenary of the death of John Wesley, the granite memorial was established on this site to reflect the work of the founder of Methodism who visited the Sandgate area in 1742 to preach in this "the poorest and most contemptible part of the town."

At the opposite end of not only the Milk Market but also the biological cycle was once the Sandgate Midden. Here the town scavenger emptied his cart of the sweepings of the streets, slaughter houses and other establishments. The contents of the midden were sold for manure and taken away either by keel or by farmer's cart.

37. The Milk Market or Sandgate pant fulfilling its purpose, c1900.

MARKETS

When Thomas Oliver wrote his *Picture of Newcastle* in 1831 he described the Milk Market as a place where "on Saturdays is a sale of old clothes laid on straw upon the street." This tradition, known as "Paddy's Market", continued, without the straw, into the second half of the twentieth century. The remains of the old Town Wall and other structures were also used for displaying wares. The area also contained a daily butcher market. The Sunday market continues to this day, perhaps now as much a tourist attraction as a place of serious trade.

39. (above) The merchandise outside Ripley's general store was clearly of interest to the bargain hunters of the turn of the century.

40. (left) By 1965 the wire coat hanger had made its impression on the scene, but little else had changed.

38. (left) Items for sale at "Paddy's Market", displayed both on the pavement and on table tops standing on trellis legs. Behind is the Lifeboat Inn and on the corner a newer building standing on the site of "The Folly". "The Folly" was built by Cuthbert Dykes in the late seventeenth century as a waterworks but the water supply scheme never came to fruition and the building eventually became a grain warehouse. This busy scene was photographed about 1900.

41. Looking down Sandgate towards Milk Market c1900.

SANDGATE

In the early nineteenth century Sandgate was described by Thomas Oliver as an old narrow street chiefly consisting of ale-houses, shops for the sale of provisions, and tenement rooms. A great number of dark, ill paved and filthy entries led from Sandgate north to the New Road (City Road) and south to Sandgate Shore. Renowned as one of the most derelict in the town the area attracted the reforming zeal of John Wesley.

It was the home of the Tyne keelmen who rowed their flat, broad-bottomed, coal-filled keel boats from the upper reaches of the river to waiting collier ships near the mouth. As early as 1736 Henry Bourne reported that "the number of souls in this Street and the Lanes belonging to it is computed to several thousands." A hundred years later Eneas Mackenzie saw the squalor of the streets and described it as the "Wapping of Newcastle".

As the power and influence of the keelmen collapsed with the loosening of their stranglehold upon the movement of coal on the river, the area fell into decline. Many people moved from the Sandgate into the newly growing suburbs and their places were taken by poor Irish workers forced off their land by the potato famines of the mid-nineteenth century. By the turn of the twentieth century the keels and the keelmen had long been a thing of the past and much of the slum housing of the area had been swept away.

42. (upper right) Barefoot children were still a common sight in 1898.

43. (right) Beds and beer on the corner of Sandgate – a bobby keeps order in 1905.

44. (left) Merchandise covers the Quayside east of the Milk Market in 1908.

SANDGATE SHORE

Running along the river's edge from the Milk Market to the Swirle and parallel to Sandgate was the Low Way, a narrow and congested street but nevertheless the principal thoroughfare of Sandgate Shore. Between it and the Sandgate itself ran dark and filthy alleys where housing and waterside industry co-existed. Beside the cramped housing of the alleys and the riverside homes of watermen, the chief occupant of the Low Way was the Tyne Brewery.

The Brewery buildings and yards ran from the Sandgate to the riverbank where the Company maintained its own wharf. The Low Way ran through the site. The road also contained a cable, chain and anchor smith's shop, a soap manufactory and a forge. All of this, however, was swept away initially by the construction of the New Quay in the 1840s and later by clearances of the old houses to make way for the warehouses and sheds which stored the many and varied cargoes which were to be shipped from the wharfs and berths of the expanding Quayside.

The Low Way, the Sandgate Midden, the forge and the Tyne Brewery had all disappeared by the 1880s.

45. A view of the same area in 1980.

46. A view across the river of the low level sheds along the quay, east of Milk Market, with the CWS warehouse rising above them to the right, c1913.

THE CWS WAREHOUSE

One of the warehouses which rose up behind the new Quayside at the turn of the twentieth century was that of the Co-operative Wholesale Society. Always progressive in its thinking, the CWS chose to build out of the very latest materials. This period saw increased use of ferro-concrete (concrete reinforced with iron) for the construction of industrial and commercial buildings. Its use was developed principally by the French engineer François Hennebique and his agent L.G. Mouchel. Mouchel's assistant, T. J. Gueritte, worked in Newcastle on the design and construction of the CWS Quayside warehouse, in conjunction with the architect F.E.L. Harris, between the years 1897 and 1900.

The site was found to have marshy silt and quicksand to a depth in places of 60ft. The building was therefore constructed on a ferro-concrete raft. The whole frame of the building was of the new material and the exterior, also of concrete, was finished to resemble the more traditional Portland stone. The architectural style chosen for the building was austere and classical. A barrel vaulted roof was added to the warehouse in 1901 bringing a decorative element to the top of the six storey building. It is now probably the oldest surviving large scale ferro-concrete building in the country.

47. The Co-operative Wholesale warehouse is at the centre of this Quayside picture from the 1980s. The image captures many of the area's most interesting buildings including the Keelmen's Hospital, the Sallyport Tower and part of the Melbourne Street Tramway Depot and Power Station.

48. The pantiled, jettied timber-framed premises of W. F. Scott stand next door to Gilroy's Spirit Vaults between Milk Market and the Swirle in 1879.

NEW AND OLD

In front of the newly built CWS warehouse lay the Hull Wharf and the Leith Wharf, both of which were developed after the Quayside extensions and improvements which began in the 1840s – although the Leith Steam Packet Office was to be found on the quay prior to this time. To the east was constructed a huge grain and general warehouse with overhead links to loading and unloading facilities at the water's edge. In between these two massively proportioned warehouses, however, a cluster of earlier buildings survived for some years.

This small group contained a metalworker's shop and a public house. W.F. Scott utilised an old pantiled timber-framed building to ply his trade as a manufacturer of ships' lamps and a worker of tin-plate. Next door stood Gilroy's Spirit Vaults, later known as the Sun Inn. In time the old timber framed building must have become unsafe or derelict for it was removed to leave what had become the Fitzgerald public house, the New Sun Inn, standing alone amidst its lofty and overbearing neighbours. This in time made way for a further brick-built warehouse constructed directly to the east of the CWS building. When this in turn was demolished in 1992 the remains of a set of limekilns, thought to be of the fourteenth century, were uncovered indicating the early industrial usage of this land outside the town walls.

49. (upper right) Fruit on sale outside the entrance to Gilroy's Spirit Vaults. Two ladies sit in the doorway of Scott's shop on a sunny day in 1885.

50. (right) By 1957 Gilroy's has become the New Sun Inn. Despite the new name the building is clearly the same. Its neighbour has gone but the convenient doorstep has survived.

THE SWIRLE

The use of the name "Swirle" has appropriately eddied to and fro about this area over the years. Originally a small stream, the name came to represent a small street which followed the line of the stream and was then later applied to the Sandgate area east of Milk Market.

The origin of the name is unclear but when Henry Bourne wrote his *History of Newcastle upon Tyne* in 1736 he explained that in the middle of Sandgate "is an open Place called the Squirrel, from a little Brook of that Name, which runs through it into the River Tyne, which was the ancient Bounds of the Town of Newcastle."

The Swirle was once important as the eastern boundary between Newcastle and the then separate township of Byker. Later it was a small but significant street containing the Half Moon Inn. The stream was crossed where it joined the river by a small wooden bridge. Here, says the historian Charleton, "sat the Sandgate lasses in their tubs, amongst the shallow water near the edge, washing tripe and singing old Newcastle ditties."

51. (left) A horse and cart stand outside the Half Moon Inn in the Swirle. At the head of the street are buildings on St Mary's Street, the eastern extension of Sandgate. The photograph dates from 1926 but the number of horse-drawn vehicles gives a Victorian atmosphere to the picture.

52. (upper right) From 1926 to 1935 the removal of its neighbour, the loss of many of the earlier architectural features and the development of new industrial buildings on St Mary's Street left the Half Moon Inn a shadow of its former self.

53. (right) The junction of the Swirle and the Quayside in 1908.

54. The Mayoral barge is lifted ashore for the last time in 1903. The then newly built CWS warehouse rises above the scene.

THE LAST BARGE

The Quayside near the Swirle saw the end of what had once been a major tradition of the river. On April 11th 1903 the Mayor's processional barge was lifted from the Tyne on to terra firma for the final time. In the early part of the nineteenth century Barge Day, when the mayor, the Master and Brethren of Trinity House and many other local worthies progressed up and down the river on a ritual tour of inspection, was a highlight of the annual calendar. The procession of brightly coloured and heavily decorated barges was accompanied by a fleet of similarly adorned small craft and by the ringing of church bells, the cheering of crowds on the riverbanks and even by the firing of cannon. The ceremonial procession began at the Mansion House Quay, sailed to the river mouth then returned upstream to Hedwin Streams. The journey was broken for refreshments at the Mansion House in The Close, (before its demise in 1835), and for entertainments on King's Meadow, the elongated island in the river at Elswick, before it too was removed later in the century. With the setting up of the Tyne Improvement Commission in 1850, the largely ceremonial annual event was abandoned and instead took place every five years until it lapsed completely, the last being in 1901.

55. (above) The final journey – bowlers and top hats for the dignitaries, boaters for the oarsmen as the ceremony comes to an end in 1901.

56. (left) The Mayoral barge waits to be hoisted ashore in 1903.

57. The forbidding bulk of the grain warehouse looms over the London Wharf in this scene from 1913.

CARGOES

Beyond the Hull Wharf and the Leith Wharf and the overhead gantries and loading chutes of the massive grain and general warehouse which dominated the centre of this stretch of Quayside lay more wharves. The London Wharf, with its substantial lattice-work timber jetty jutting into the river, the Hamburg and Rotterdam Wharves all marked the historic trading links with the capital and the continent. Newer trading partners were represented by the Antwerp and Malmo Wharfs.

" It is an interesting sight to see the steamers arrive and discharge their cargoes on the quay. There are baskets of fruit and potatoes by the thousand; there is hay and moss litter, cheese, butter, and eggs, bacon and lard, and flour, besides many other food supplies. Then there is the live stock – pigs, loudly protesting, and sheep, quietly and gently being driven on shore; while great droves of cattle are hustled and prodded, and beaten and dragged and hurried off to their various destinations. Most interesting of all is to see the Scandinavian emigrants, who arrive every week on their way to that land of promise, America." (Charleton, 1885).

58. A Quayside crane rises above the Antwerp, Hamburg and Rotterdam Wharf in April 1913.

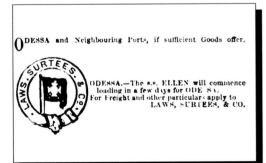

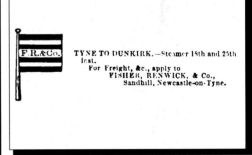

Advertisements from *The Tyne Bill of Entry and Shipping List*, Thursday, July 17, 1879.

59. A Quayside Railway scene of 1909, with part of the 80 ton crane on the right.

TRACKS AND TUNNELS

The Quayside Railway line serving the warehouses, wharves and manufactories along the river frontage was first planned in 1845 but the 1 in 30 gradient was too steep for the locomotives of the time. The railway, which was almost semi-circular in plan and connected the quay to Manors Station, was however finally opened on the 1st June 1870.

The construction of the line involved the resculpturing of Ropery Banks and the digging of the Lime Street cutting. A large and impressive masonry retaining wall held back the cut-away Ropery Banks and a steeply graded tunnel carried the track up and away from the quay to join the North Eastern Railway line at the Trafalgar Street Sidings. The ascent from the Quayside was so steep that engines suffered wheel-slip and the amount of impetus required to power the locomotives up the hill was so great that the tunnel quickly became smoke-filled and made the task of driving both unhealthy and difficult.

Two special locomotives were built in 1904 to overcome these difficulties following the electrification of the system. The line worked until 16th June 1969 after which the cutting was filled in and the tunnel entrances blocked. The Quayside entrance to the railway tunnel had been through a still visible portal behind the Hamburg Wharf.

The railway along the quay was constructed by the Corporation but the expensive and elaborate connection to the main line was the work of the NER. The task was made more difficult by having to cross above the line of the second subterranean structure in the area – the Victoria Tunnel.

The Victoria Tunnel emerged on to the Quayside to the west of the mouth of the Ouseburn. This remarkable structure – a tunnel over two miles in length running under the heart of Newcastle – was opened in 1842 to carry coals on an underground railway from the newly opened Spital Tongues Colliery to staiths at the riverside.

60. By the summer of 1910 the construction of the new retaining wall on Ropery Banks was well under way.

The tunnel, having passed under the northern part of the town and parts of Sandyford, descended sharply from New Bridge Street, crossed under Lime Street and emerged on a raised timber staith over the river. The enterprise was, however, short lived and the tunnel mouth and the staiths were swept away following the closure of the Colliery in 1857 and the construction of Glasshouse Bridge in 1878.

61. Although the Quayside Railway left the quay at the west end of Ropery Banks, the line itself continued along the river's edge to the Malmo Wharf at the mouth of the Ouseburn. This scene in September 1909 shows the complicated task of demolishing and rebuilding the retaining wall by Horatio Street.

THE NORTH SHORE

The North Shore encompassed the riverside from the Swirle to the mouth of the Ouseburn and included the long mound known as Ropery Banks. The mound was thought to be the first of the ballast hills, created by the dumping of waste material brought as ballast by collier ships coming into the Tyne, which developed along this stretch of the river.

Whilst the raised terrain became the home of the St Ann's Ropery, a windmill and in time a number of manufacturing works, the riverside developed as the centre of the town's shipbuilding and repairing industry. Until the quay extensions and improvements of the mid-nineteenth century took place the North Shore was home to several early shipyards: Farrington's Shipyard which stood at the foot of Wide Open, (one of the streets running from Sandgate to the shore), Hopper's Yard, Fulton's Yard, Hopper's Slipway, Wright's Yard and at the mouth of the Ouseburn another of Hopper's Yards. Also here was the "Dandy Gears" – a timber coal staith with three spouts which transferred coal brought from Shieldfield into collier ships or into waiting keels for shipment to the river mouth.

The early history of this area as a ballast hill is recorded in Gray's *Survey of Newcastle upon Tyne* in 1649 where he says "women upon their heads carried ballast, which was taken forth of small ships which came empty for coales." By the beginning of the nineteenth century the less precipitous slopes were crowded with houses and shops. Above these stood the rope works of the Crawhall family. Joseph Crawhall purchased the St Ann's Ropery in 1835 and later constructed a remarkable chimney in the shape of a rope-end which rose above his works and became a landmark of the area.

Next door to the ropery was a brush works. Ships' chandlers, block and mast makers, carvers, painters and other ship-related trades grew up to serve the riverside yards below. There was also, according to Charleton, a huge windlass which stood in the garden of the Golden Lion and was used for drawing ships up Hopper's Slipway.

62. The Hope and Anchor – pictured here on 15th December 1909 – was at hand to supply refreshment to the thirsty workforce.

63. Work on the quay extension at the mouth of the Ouseburn, pictured on 2nd October 1907. To the right of the crane is the Sailor's Bethel, a non-conformist chapel built in 1875, now converted to offices and meeting rooms. Running up the hill adjacent to the chapel was Tyne Street, at the bottom of which was the Lamb Inn and at the top, the Golden Lion.

THE OUSEBURN

"We are now in a truly desolate-looking region" (Charleton, 1885)

At the eastern end of the North Shore is the mouth of the Ouseburn and the intriguing blend of housing and industry which forms the lower Ouseburn valley.

The development of the lower Ouseburn Valley has been in sharp contrast to the sylvan stretches of the river which flow through Jesmond Dene and Heaton. Whereas the whole valley had once been predominantly agricultural and is thought to have taken its name from a corruption of "Ewes Burn", the lower part of the valley became one of the cradles of industrialisation in the region. The faster flowing sections of the upper reaches led to the use of the water to power corn mills in a number of locations. Some of these, in later years, were altered to grind flint for the pottery industry of the area. The combination of water power, easy access to the Tyne, raw material in the ever-growing ballast hills and the location beyond the inhibiting walls of the late medieval town fostered the early growth of industrial activity.

In the upper Ouseburn the eighteenth and nineteenth century mills gave way to the development of the Victorian parks of Jesmond Dene, Heaton and Armstrong Parks, but nearer to the mouth potteries, glassworks, mills (corn, flour, flax, flint, and spinning), leadworks, soapworks, glue and copperas manufactories, foundries, roperies and small shipbuilding yards all grew up within the confines of the valley.

The many works and the wretched conditions of some of the streets led to the disparaging comments of the historians Mackenzie and Charleton.

"A Plebeian district covered with extensive and important manufactories, consisting of corn steam-mills, foundries, potteries, a flaxmill and other works …" (Mackenzie, 1827)

"We find it, black and sullen, flowing among the most forbidding surroundings. Slaughter-houses, coal wharves and dwelling houses of not the most desirable appearance … keels may be seen lying and

delivering coal into carts, which are backed axle-deep into the stream to receive their load, while the horses stand impatiently in the cold water. In the cold water too we see groups of ragged people with baskets and bags, wading and groping with their hands for the coal which has fallen overboard." (Charleton, 1885)

64. Housing was as much a part of the Ouseburn Valley as industry. Here children congregate at the rear of 12, Ouse Street and in Mordue's Yard, off Cut Bank, in 1935.

65. By January 1908 the demolition of the old Glasshouse Bridge was underway.

THE GLASSHOUSE BRIDGES

William Gray writing in his *Survey of Newcastle upon Tyne* in 1649 says that "upon the north side of the river is the Ewes Burn, over which is a wood bridge, which goeth down to a place called the Glasse Houses where plaine glasse for windowes are made which serveth most parts of the Kingdom." This early Glasshouse Bridge was replaced in stone in 1669 by Thomas Wrangham, a renowned Newcastle shipbuilder. Wrangham's bridge was altered and made level and more convenient in 1727 but still retained a striking and pleasant appearance, giving an almost romantic look to the mouth of the burn.

The more prosaic but more practical high level Glasshouse Bridge was constructed to the north of the old bridge in the late 1870s and linked what is now City Road with Walker Road. The seventeenth century stone bridge was dismantled during the extension of the Quayside in the years between 1907 and 1910.

66 (above) A mid-nineteenth century view of the eighteenth century Glasshouse Bridge.

67. (left) Despite the many alterations to the area near the mouth of the Ouseburn the Glasshouse Bridge, the low level pipe-bridge and the Ship Tavern, all visible in this picture from 1906, still survive.

EAST OF OUSEBURN

The area immediately east of the mouth of the Ouseburn, stretching along the Tyne to the old Corporation boundary with St Peter's Parish, was known as St Lawrence. It was one of four areas which formed the south side of Byker township, the others being St Ann's, St Peter's and St Anthony's. The St Lawrence area was based upon the chapel of St Lawrence, said to date from the early thirteenth century.

The earliest signs of industrial development can be traced to the early seventeenth century. From 1619 and possibly earlier, Sir Robert Mansell, the Vice-Admiral of England, had been establishing glass-houses on the Tyne on land in St Lawrence leased from the Corporation. By the late eighteenth century the site of the chapel had been subsumed within one of the glassworks.

The St Lawrence glass industry was, perhaps, the most significant early glass-making site in the country. The attractions of the area lay in the plentiful supply of coal and the easy access to regular shipping traffic to London and other ports. In 1635 King Charles I prohibited the import of any sort of glass from abroad during the term granted by King James I to Mansell for the sole making of glass. By the mid-seventeenth century there were three sets of works established in this area, after which the industry spread to other parts of the river – Howdon Pans, Bill Quay and Close Gate.

By the 1770s it was reported that fifteen large glass works (one for plate glass, three crown glass houses, five for broad or common window glass, two for white or flint glass and five bottle houses) were situated on the Tyne in and around Newcastle – the cluster at St Lawrence being the earliest and largest.

68, 69, 70. Three views showing the area immediately east of the Ouseburn. These buildings included the River Police Station and the Dead House, where grappling irons were kept to remove bodies from the river and where the bodies were laid out. These pictures date from 1906, just a few months before their demolition as part of the extension work.

THE INDUSTRIAL DEVELOPMENT OF ST LAWRENCE 1770 - 1900

By the time of Hutton's map of Newcastle in 1772, the area was dominated by the High, Middle and Low Glasshouses, the only other industry noted being a ropery. By the 1830s and 1840s some housing had grown up around the three glass manufactories and the ropery had developed into an enclosed building, some of which survives today. The industrial intensity of the site had grown by this period and by the late 1850s a number of uses had developed.

From the mouth of the Ouseburn to the Mushroom Bottle Works were an iron foundry, a fire-brick manufactory, a pottery, a bottle manufactory (the High Glass Houses), a broad and crown glass works, the Tyne Manure and Chemical Works, St Lawrence Ironworks, St Lawrence Ropery, St Lawrence Steam Saw Mill, timber yards, shipbuilding yards and some dwellings.

By the end of the nineteenth century large complexes dominated the area – the St Lawrence Bottle Works, the Ironworks, Ropeworks, Manure Works and the Saw Mill had grown as the glass industry (other than the bottle works) and the pottery and chemical industries contracted.

The riverside itself, however, clearly retained a certain charm for some. Charleton described it as smoke-blackened and neglected whilst commenting on its appearance as old-fashioned and picturesque: "We find ourselves," he observed, "amongst a crowd of old brick buildings, huddled together without regard to order." Prominent amongst these were the River Police Station and next door the "Dead House" where bodies hauled from the river were laid to rest.

72. Further extensions east of Ouseburn spelled the end of this striking landmark at Carr's Timber Yard. The felling of the chimney, captured here, took place on January 16th 1931.

71. (left) The Quayside extension works involved the removal of this chimney at the St Lawrence Bottle Works in the summer of 1908.

73. Spiller's Tyne Mill, pictured here in 1940 two years after completion, stands only yards from the former site of the Mushroom Hotel.

QUAYSIDE EXTENSIONS AND IMPROVEMENTS

In the first decade of the twentieth century extensive and ambitious alterations were proposed by the City Engineer for a considerable length of the river frontage, including the extension of the quay east of the Ouseburn into the St Lawrence area.

A substantial part of the City Engineer's proposals were acted upon, although the work in the St Lawrence area was not carried out to its full extent until later in the century.

Prior to this time there was little open space on the river frontage. The terrain, which had previously sloped down to the river, was cut into by the twentieth century developments and the large retaining wall at the rear of the quay was built as part of these alterations.

The principle clearing of the quay area did not take place until the 1930s. It is possible that the expiry of the lease of the saw mill in 1935 was the catalyst for this activity. Sheds of the type envisaged in 1903 were constructed to add to that which had been built immediately to the east of the mouth of the Ouseburn as part of the Norway Wharf. Most importantly for the development of the area, the Spiller's Mill was started at this time.

Spiller's Tyne Mill was completed in 1938 and was, then, the tallest flour milling building in the world. Spiller's had come to Newcastle in 1896, when they acquired Davidson's Phoenix Mill in The Close. The Tyne Mill replaced this older complex. There were two main buildings at the Tyne Mill – the Silo and the Flour Mill. The Silo was designed to store 34,000 tons of grain. The mill contained a warehouse, the flour mill and an animal food mill. To serve it the deep water berth was improved and the rail network along the Quayside extended.

74. Half a century earlier than the photograph of Spiller's Mill, the scene is strikingly different. An air of old world charm pervades this picture of the Mushroom Hotel and landing taken in 1886, probably hiding a less picturesque reality.

ALL CHANGE

The Quayside has changed considerably over the centuries. The improvements and extensions carried out throughout the nineteenth and early twentieth centuries were designed to create more and better docking and loading facilities to foster the trade of the river. The economic changes of the the second half of the twentieth century have rendered these facilities redundant and long stretches of the quay obsolete. The alteration and redesigning of the area in the 1990s is creating a new Quayside where leisure and recreation are part of the economic and social mix.

The completion of Spiller's Mill in 1938 was the last major industrial innovation on Newcastle's historic Quayside. The climactic change which was to occur on the waterfront, however, had been signalled ten years earlier with the opening of the new Tyne Bridge. The economic artery of the region and the proud symbol of the City was no longer the river but the bridge which crossed it.

75. (left) The Stone Cellers Inn, as its curiously spelled nameboard announces in this picture of 1879, was made famous by Ralph Hedley as the subject of his painting "Weary Waiting" and was described in glorious detail and atmosphere by Charleton:

" An old public house well known in Newcastle as the scene of so many inquests on bodies found on the Tyne ... There is the bar, with its sanded floor, and behind it the usual high altar of Bacchus ... a kitchen with a huge fire-place, sanded floor, long-settles, spittoons and other accessories ... a dark staircase ascending to unknown regions above, and guarded by a portcullis sort of gate, made of jet-black oak ... a cell-like chamber with a bench down each side, taking up what room is not occupied by the table ... the parlour, its low ceiling which can be easily touched by hand ... Down a few steps in one corner you come to a door, and, opening it, step out upon a wooden gallery overhanging the river. Leaning on the railing of the gallery we see the little wooden dead-house – seldom without some silent occupant."

(Charleton, 1885)

76. The first building of the East Quayside redevelopment scheme of the 1990s takes shape in the shadow of the CWS warehouse – the only industrial structure to survive from the many past developments of this stretch of the waterfront.

BRIEF BIBLIOGRAPHY

There are surprisingly few readily available histories of Newcastle upon Tyne. Sidney Middlebrook's book, first published in 1950, is still the most useful and generally reliable source. A recent general history, published by Northern Heritage, offers a lively and popular approach to the subject. The works of the historians Charleton and Mackenzie and the architect-surveyor Thomas Oliver provide valuable contemporary evidence of the growth of the town in the nineteenth century. Similarly the eighteenth century picture portrayed in the books by Henry Bourne and John Brand and the information contained in Gray's writings in 1649 are particularly interesting. The maps drawn up by James Corbridge in 1723-4, by Charles Hutton in 1770, Thomas Oliver in 1830 and 1844 and by the Ordnance Survey in the 1850s and 1890s also provide essential information to anyone interested in the historical development of the town and the Quayside. Of the more detailed studies of the Quayside, the most recent publication on its early development has been carried out by Colm O'Brien. In addition Newcastle City Libraries and Arts have produced a number of local history publications. Many other detailed and specific articles and books about the area can be consulted within the Local Studies Section of the Central Library.

DETAILS:

Bourne, H. *The History of Newcastle upon Tyne*, 1736. Reprinted 1980.

Brand, J. *The History and Antiquities of the Town and County of Newcastle upon Tyne*, 1789.

Charleton, R.J. *Newcastle Town*, 1885. Reprinted in 1989 as *A History of Newcastle-on-Tyne* .

Gray, W. *Chorographia; or a Survey of Newcastle upon Tyne*, 1649. Reprinted 1970.

Mackenzie, E. *A Descriptive and Historical account of the Town and County of Newcastle upon Tyne*, 1827.

Middlebrook, S. *Newcastle upon Tyne: Its Growth and Achievement,* 1950. Second Edition 1968.

O'Brien, C. et al. *The Origins of the Newcastle Quayside,* 1988.

Oliver, T. *A New Picture of Newcastle upon Tyne,* 1831. Reprinted 1970.

Winter, P. et al. *Northern Heritage: Newcastle upon Tyne,* 1989.